LOS GATOS PUBLIC LIBRARY
Telephone: 408-354-6891

A fine shall be charged each day an item is kept overtime. No item will be issued to persons in arrears for fines.

Loss of, or damage to an item other than regular wear and tear, must be paid by the person to whom the book is charged.

Attention is called to the rule that items borrowed from the library must not be loaned.

For violation of these rules, the privileges of the library may be withdrawn from any person at any time.

GAYLORD F

Nature's Children

WORKING DOGS

Edward C. Haggerty

Grolier Educational

FACTS IN BRIEF

Classification of the Domestic Dog

Class: *Mammalia* (mammals)

Order: *Carnivora* (meat eaters)

Family: *Canidae* (dogs, wolves, foxes, jackals)

Genus: *Canis* (dogs)

Species: *Canis familiaris* (the domestic dog)

World distribution. All countries.

Habitat. Everywhere humans are found.

Distinctive physical characteristics. Differences in dogs' bodies come from selective breeding. Most dogs have long, slender legs, a long skull, and a muscular, deep-chested body. Depending on the breed, adult dogs weigh anywhere from 4 to 220 pounds (2 to 99 kilograms) and stand 5 to 35 inches tall (12.5 to 89 centimeters).

Habits. In the wild dogs live and hunt in packs that have an established social structure. Domestic dogs transfer pack loyalty to their human owners and families.

Diet. Dogs have a simple carnivore (flesh-eating) stomach. They can eat cooked vegetables and grain as well as meat.

Library of Congress Cataloging-in-Publication

Haggerty, Edward C., 1946-
   Working dogs / Edward C. Haggerty
        p.   cm. — (Nature's children)
   Includes index.
   Summary: Describes distinctive physical characteristics, behavior,
distribution throughout the world, and diet of these animals which
are employed in various ways.
   ISBN 0-7172-9123-5 (hardbound)
   1. Working dogs—Juvenile literature.   [1.Working dogs.
2. Dogs.]   I. Title.   II. Series.   97-5974
SF428.5.H34 1997   CIP
636.73—dc21   AC

This library reinforced edition was published in 1997 exclusively by:

 Grolier Educational

Sherman Turnpike, Danbury, Connecticut 06816

Set ISBN 0-7172-7661-9
Working Dogs ISBN 0-7172-9123-5

Contents

Canines in Blue	Page 6
Specialized Police Work	Page 9
Schutzhund Competitions	Page 10
Dogs to the Rescue	Page 12
Bloodhounds on the Trail	Page 15
Not by Scent Alone	Page 16
Mush!	Page 18
The Iditarod	Page 20
Herding Dogs	Page 22
Instinct and Training	Page 24
International Sheepdog Trials	Page 26
Natural Born Hunters	Page 27
From Sporting Dogs to Pets	Page 29
Its Name Makes You Think of . . .	Page 30
They're Off!	Page 32
Guide Dogs for the Blind	Page 34
Training Guide Dogs	Page 37
A Remarkable Partnership	Page 38
Service Dogs	Page 40
Therapy Dogs	Page 42
Dog Stars	Page 43
The Championship Trail	Page 45
Dogs for All Seasons	Page 46
Words to Know	Page 47
Index	Page 48

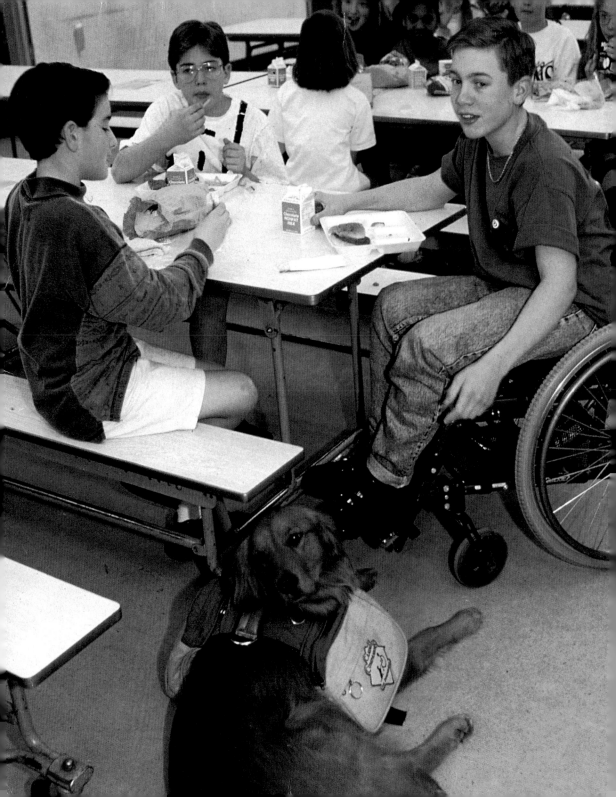

Fifty million dogs live in the United States. But that should come as no surprise. After all, dogs and humans have lived side by side, as partners, for over 10,000 years.

Somewhere, long ago, in a dark forest or on a cold, open plain, a hungry wolf or fox pup wandered into a hunter's camp in search of food. That pup, which earned its food by guarding the camp or helping with the hunt, became the ancestor of the modern dog.

As time passed, humans realized that all dogs were not the same. Some dogs had great strength and endurance; others were swift runners or fierce fighters. In time people bred dogs to develop particular traits, providing themselves with canine hunters, herders, and guards.

Over the years people also learned that many of the traits that made good working dogs also made good helping dogs. Today these service dogs are the eyes, ears, and close companions that help their owners lead independent and productive lives.

For thousands of years dogs have given help
to people who need it.

Canines in Blue: Dogs in Law Enforcement

One of the main areas in which dogs work today is law enforcement. Police departments use K-9, or canine, units to search for suspects and to protect citizens, while private companies use dogs to provide security for stores, factories, and warehouses. Dogs help the armed forces guard military bases, and dogs aid the Secret Service in protecting the president, first family, and other important officials.

Regardless of exactly what they do, law enforcement dogs need to be strong, intelligent, and obedient. And they must trust—and be trusted by—their handlers.

To build a strong bond between them, handlers and dogs train together, learning to work as a team. Many dogs even live with their handler's families as pets. As a result, handlers and law enforcement dogs are able to trust each other in different situations and can depend completely on each other's skill, judgment, and strength.

German shepherds make ideal law enforcement dogs.

Specialized Police Work

Trained police dogs can run faster and hear better than their human handlers. They can crawl through tighter spaces and sniff out hidden suspects better, too.

Because of these abilities, some police dogs get special tasks to do. Many of these jobs are in airports, where local police and airport security units protect travelers from dangers of all kinds.

At a large number of airports dogs use their keen sense of smell to search out explosives in airport cargo areas, terminals, and aircraft. Once they find them, bomb squads can remove the explosives before any harm can be done.

Dogs have also been trained to find illegal drugs and locate chemicals that arsonists use to start fires. At international airports dogs search travelers' luggage to sniff out plants and foods that might be carrying harmful organisms from one country to another.

K-9 dogs train long and hard.

Schutzhund Competitions

What is work for one person—or dog—is sport and fun for another. There are, for example, pilots who fly as a job; there are also pilots who fly just for fun. In the world of police dogs and guard dogs there is a competitive sport called Schutzhund.

Schutzhund is a German word that means "protection dog." But it is also a rapidly growing sport that tests a dog's discipline and obedience. In addition, it tests a dog's mastery of tracking, guard dog skills, and what is called bitework.

Schutzhund dogs are powerful animals with lots of energy and drive. The dogs most commonly used are rottweilers, boxers, Doberman pinschers, and other aggressive breeds.

Strength and aggression are not everything in Schutzhund, however. The real object of Schutzhund is to train calm, reliable dogs that are always under control. Dogs that are nervous or that cannot stop an attack on command are eliminated from training and competition.

Schutzhund dogs attack— and stop—on command.

Dogs to the Rescue

Day-hikers fail to return on time. A building collapses, and people are trapped somewhere in the rubble. A young child wanders off and cannot be found. In real life unfortunate events like this happen, and when they do, authorities often call in search and rescue (SAR) dogs.

Some SAR dogs work full time with a local police force; others simply are the talented, well-trained pets of civilian volunteers. Regardless, these dogs rely on two main ways to follow a person's trail—tracking and trailing. When dogs track, they follow a person's exact path, following footprints and other clues. When they trail, they follow a person's scent.

Many SAR dogs are so good at their jobs that they can trail people who are in cars, following the scent that blows out of the vehicle's vents and windows. Not even water stops a good SAR dog. If the water is calm, the dog can follow the person's scent right across the surface. If the water is rough, the canine simply swims to the other side and sniffs until it picks up the person's scent once again!

Search and rescue dogs stand ready to help.

Bloodhounds on the Trail

Movies and TV programs often show howling bloodhounds following the trail of an escaped prisoner or a lost child. The truth is that bloodhounds usually are silent when they track. Still, bloodhounds are the best tracking dogs in the world, stubbornly following a trail that is miles long and hours old.

How do bloodhounds manage to locate people? People's scents are as unique as fingerprints, and wherever they go, people leave an invisible trail of scent behind them. Sometimes, but not often, people can smell this trail. Dogs—especially bloodhounds— can identify it easily.

To help in the search, the dog's handler finds something touched or worn by the person for whom they will be searching. The handler has the dog smell that object to pick up the person's scent. Even if the object has been handled by several people, a well-trained dog will be able to follow the scent of the person in question.

SAR dogs often take to the water.

Not by Scent Alone

Not all searches by dogs involve trailing a particular scent. SAR dogs also rescue people lost in the wilderness, buried by avalanches and earthquakes, or even trapped by airplane crashes and other disasters. In cases like these the rescue dogs are not looking for any person in particular. Instead, they are sniffing the air and following any human scent they find.

Whatever task they are doing, SAR teams try to match the job to the dog. Bloodhounds work best on a leash, so trailing searches are ideal jobs for them. Disaster searches, however, need dogs like Labradors and German shepherds that work easily off the leash. More agile than bloodhounds, they can scramble, climb, and dig with ease.

For work in snow there are always the famous Saint Bernards. Hardy enough to endure terrible cold—and to make their way through high snow drifts—these courageous dogs have saved countless climbers and skiers in the Swiss Alps and other mountains.

St. Bernards have made many mountain rescues.

Mush!

Sled dogs may be the best known of all working dogs. Today the people of Alaska and northern Canada travel the back country by snowmobile. But long before there was the snowmobile there was the sled, which was pulled by teams of dogs.

Sled dogs are usually huskies, malamutes, or Samoyeds, and they are born with a strong urge to pull and run. They would rather run in the bitter cold than stay by a warm fire. They are also very strong. In pulling competitions a 60-pound (27-kilogram) dog has pulled as much as 2,000 pounds (900 kilograms).

Most dog teams are made up of five, seven, or nine dogs. The lead dog is the most important. The rest of the team is hitched in pairs behind it. The lead dog regulates speed and direction for the entire team. The musher, or driver, uses voice commands—like the traditional cry of "Mush!"—to make the dog team speed up, slow down, and turn.

Sled dogs were born to pull and run.

The Iditarod

At one time dogsleds carried mail, supplies, and people over a system of Alaskan trails that stretched more than 2,000 miles (3,220 kilometers). Today, however, dogsledding is more a sport than anything else.

The most famous dogsled race is the Iditarod, which is officially known as the Iditarod Trail Sled Dog Race. Run on an 1,100-mile (1,771-kilometer) course between Anchorage and Nome, Alaska, the Iditarod takes anywhere from 11 to 21 days to complete. During that time drivers and dog teams face harsh winter weather, rugged terrain, and even wild animals.

The Iditarod race was begun to honor the heroic efforts of dog teams and drivers who saved the city of Nome in January 1925. At that time Nome was threatened by an epidemic of the deadly disease diphtheria. Bad weather kept even aircraft from getting life-saving vaccine to the city. Only Alaska's traditional dogsleds, braving the cold and snow, were able to make it through to the city.

Sled dog races are hard work but exciting.

Herding Dogs

People have raised cattle and sheep for more than 9,000 years. These animals have often been led, protected, and kept together by working dogs.

Over thousands of years many dogs have been bred especially for their herding skills, and each breed has its own style of working. Rottweilers, which first herded cattle for the ancient Romans, butt the cattle to push them along. Small, fast corgis dart in and out of the herd, nipping at the cattle's heels.

Border collies work differently. They control sheep with a steady, hypnotizing stare that breeders call "eye." In contrast, Old English sheepdogs use no "eye" at all. Instead, they drive sheep along by barking.

Australian kelpies have one of the most unusual herding methods of all. Working in crowded pens, kelpies "woolwalk" along the sheep's backs. Then they jump into the milling flock to clear tangles of sheep.

Dogs have protected sheep for thousands of years.

Instinct and Training

Sheepherding is the perfect pairing of the basic instincts of sheep and sheepdog. Sheep want to follow a leader and stay together in a flock. Sheepdogs want to herd those sheep, just as their ancestors have done for centuries.

As soon as a sheltie or border collie can walk, it will try to herd anything that moves. People, insects, pets, and even leaves are all likely candidates. But the dog isn't a real sheepdog yet. That takes serious training.

Training starts when the dog is about six months old. At first the dog works with just a few sheep, learning to respond to the shepherd's voice and hand signals.

After a while the young dog is taught to round up strays and guide a flock to different ground. In a few more months the dog finally learns to herd sheep into a pen and to separate particular sheep from the flock for shearing, medical help, and other needs. By then the new sheepdog is ready for a flock of its own.

This corgi will bring this sheep back to the herd.

International Sheepdog Trials

A shepherd and a trained sheepdog work as a team. They work so closely that the best teams seem to read each other's minds. That's when they're ready to enter the sheepdog trials.

Sheepdog trials are contests that test speed, skill, and teamwork. National contests are held in North and South America, Europe, and Australia. International sheepdog trials are for the best of the best.

Winning an international championship is not easy. The winning dog must control more sheep at greater distances and in more complex ways than in the national contests. Here's what happens.

A whistle or voice command from its handler sends a dog racing 750 yards (683 meters) toward a group of 20 sheep. The dog must drive the sheep through a complicated series of gates and pens. Judges rate contestants on their speed and style, as well as on the number of commands they need to complete the job. The winner is the best sheepdog in the world!

Natural Born Hunters

First bred to help human hunters find and bring back game, hunting dogs also make good pets—if they get enough exercise.

Pointers get their name from how they use their bodies to point to game. When a pointer scents game, it stands completely still. Then it bends one leg, extends its tail, and stares in the direction of the animal it has found.

Setters once were trained to crouch, or set, when they found game. Today they are usually trained to point instead.

Retrievers are another useful helper for human hunters. These dogs fetch, or retrieve, the game that hunters kill. The dogs pick up the game—usually birds or small animals—and gently carry it back to the hunter in their mouths.

Some dogs, like golden retrievers, are bred for work in fields, meadows, and forests. Others work in and around lakes, ponds, and even oceans. Labrador retrievers, for example, love swimming so much that they happily jump into the very coldest water.

This German shorthaired pointer shows the hunter just where the game will be found.

From Sporting Dogs to Pets

Many other breeds began their history as hunting dogs, bred to have just the right body and temperament for specific hunting tasks.

Today a dachshund's low-slung body makes most people think of a hot dog on legs. But dachshunds first were bred to hunt small burrowing animals like badgers. The dachshunds' small body and short legs let the dogs chase their prey right down into the animals' underground homes.

Terriers range in size from the 10-pound (4.5-kilogram) Scottie to the 55-pound (25-kilogram) Airedale. Most people think of these dogs as pets. But terriers have long been famous as fierce, determined hunters of rabbits, foxes, badgers, and rats.

Even poodles were hunters in their early days. The puffy haircuts that decorate today's poodles actually come from their early days as retrievers. At that time the fur on poodles' legs was shaved off to help the dogs swim faster. The hair on their chests and heads was left long to keep the dogs warm in cold water.

Its Name Makes You Think of . . .

What comes to mind when you hear the word dalmatian? Most people think "firehouse" because these spotted dogs have been known as firehouse dogs for more than a century.

Originally dalmatians were bred in Europe as hunting dogs. In England owners found that sleek, swift dalmatians made excellent carriage dogs. Trotting alongside—or even underneath—horses and coaches, the dalmatians warned drivers of approaching bandits and alerted pedestrians to the racing carriage.

Dalmatians came to North America back when horses still pulled fire engines. Because these fast, fearless dogs could keep up with racing fire engines, dalmatians soon were adopted by fire departments from coast to coast.

Today dalmatians are no longer on active duty. But many firehouses still keep these dogs around as warmhearted mascots.

Dalmatians still are beloved firehouse pets.

They're Off!

Some hunting dogs find their prey by scent. Greyhounds, borzoi, Afghan hounds, and whippets, on the other hand, rely on keen eyesight to catch their prey. For this reason these breeds sometimes are called sighthounds.

Greyhounds, which have a history going back to ancient Egypt, are elegant, graceful dogs; they also are extremely fast. In short bursts they can reach speeds up to 50 miles (80 kilometers) an hour.

Because of greyhounds' speed, people eventually began to race them, and the sport of dog racing has been active for more than 400 years. Today organized greyhound racing is controversial because a number of people consider it cruel and inhumane. Still, in many parts of North America it is extremely popular, drawing thousands of fans to see each set of races.

Racing greyhounds reach speeds of 50 miles (80 kilometers) per hour.

Guide Dogs for the Blind

Most dogs strain against the leash when they are walked. By nature dogs want to explore and roam. Not so guide dogs. When these German shepherds, Labradors, and golden retrievers walk, they are on duty. They remain calm, obedient, and watchful regardless of what is happening around them. That they act this way is important. Their owner's safety is at stake.

Guide dogs help blind people go just about anywhere sighted people can go. In fact, guide dogs are so important and so special that they are protected by law. No one may prevent a guide dog and owner from entering any public place—even if regular dogs aren't allowed there.

Guide dogs have many responsibilities. They guide their owners on sidewalks, across streets, and down stairs. They even keep track of obstacles like doorways, curbs, and low-hanging light fixtures. It is no wonder that everyone—from the dogs and their owners to the people who train them—think that guide dogs are nothing short of amazing!

Dogs can take blind people almost anywhere.

Training Guide Dogs

Guide dogs must be intelligent, patient, and tireless workers. They also need to be large enough to wear heavy harnesses on their backs. But at the same time, guide dogs need to be small enough not to get in the way in stores, classrooms, and other crowded places.

Dogs that will become guide dogs are picked as puppies. To make sure that only the most suitable dogs are chosen, many guide dog organizations breed their own puppies. These puppies then spend their early months in foster homes with families who volunteer to take care of them.

The families teach the puppies basic obedience and good manners, while also helping the dogs become comfortable around people. After a year and a half the dogs move on to their formal training.

The dogs go to school for six months or more. During that time they learn how to lead a person, recognize obstacles and problems, and maneuver on streets and sidewalks.

Training guide dogs is a long, difficult job.

A Remarkable Partnership

Guide dogs and their masters have a remarkable partnership. To make it successful, both dogs and humans must work to build—and maintain—feelings of cooperation and trust.

The groups that provide guide dogs try to make it as easy as possible for new owners to work with a dog. Dogs and owners spend several weeks training together, supervised by an experienced instructor. Together they practice going to stores and riding buses, crossing streets, and anything else the owner regularly does.

When the instructor finally thinks both dog and master are ready, they "solo." As the instructor watches, the two go out and navigate the world on their own.

Dogs and owners remain partners for eight to ten years. By then a guide dog is ready to retire. Dogs go to carefully chosen homes with loving volunteer families, while owners get new canine companions and friends.

Guide dogs and their owners are devoted partners.

Service Dogs

These days, dogs—especially Labrador and golden retrievers, German shepherds, corgis, and border collies—are also being trained to help humans who have other kinds of problems.

Signal dogs are trained to help people who have severe hearing difficulties. Becoming their owners' ears, these dogs alert their masters to important sounds. If the telephone rings, a dog will go back and forth between the phone and its owner, leading its owner to the source of the sound. A dog will even let its owner know about a ringing doorbell, crying baby, or buzzing smoke alarm!

Other service dogs are trained to assist people who are unable to use their arms or legs. The dogs can retrieve out-of-reach clothing and, with the aid of a rope handle, open a door. They can even pull on a cord and turn on an electric light. In fact, there is little that these canine helpers cannot do for their masters.

Dogs can perform many different services.

Therapy Dogs

Do you have a dog or a cat at home? Or do you have some other soft, cuddly pet? If you do, you know how calm you feel when you stroke the animal's fur. Pets often have that effect on people.

People who are in nursing homes, hospitals, and long-term care programs can get lonely. Visits with other people cheer them up. But so do visits with animals that are brought to the facilities by volunteer owners. Dogs in programs like this are called therapy dogs.

Not every dog can be a therapy dog, of course. The dogs chosen must be gentle and calm. And they must go through special training programs to make sure that their behavior will not upset the people they are visiting. Training programs for pets and owners are available at many hospitals, nursing homes, and other facilities.

Dog Stars

Dogs have been performers and entertainers for countless years. They have been clowns and trapeze artists in circuses and acrobats on stage. They have starred in everything from movies and TV shows to commercials.

The dogs who starred as Shadow and Chance in the *Homeward Bound* movies were an American bulldog named Petey and a golden retriever named Clovis. Each of these dogs actually had stand-ins, just like human movie stars. The stand-ins were used for stunt scenes and anything else that might tire the "star."

The makers of the 1996 movie *101 Dalmatians* faced a special problem, though. Naturally, the puppies grew bigger while the movie was being filmed. So several young dogs were needed to play each of the six main puppies in the film. To make the puppies look alike, makeup artists had to add spots to some dogs and cover spots on others.

The Championship Trail

Some dogs are champions not because they catch criminals or win dogsled races but because their bloodlines are right. These are the dogs that win the "best of breed" awards. Many of them are professional show dogs, and some are worth a fortune to breeders of champion dogs.

In the United States the American Kennel Club (or AKC) officially recognizes 130 different breeds of dogs, and it sets standards for each breed. These standards tell exactly what the "ideal" collie, German shepherd, or other purebred dog should be. Covering everything important about a dog, these standards describe the dog's size and shape, the color, markings, and feel of its coat, and even how the dog should move and behave.

Judges at an official AKC dog show study the dogs and decide how close each dog comes to the standards set for that breed. Then the judges give points—and award ribbons—to the dogs that come closest to the standards.

Show dogs are carefully groomed before each contest.

Dogs for All Seasons

Dogs and humans have been together for thousands and thousands of years. During most of that time dogs have had to earn their places in people's hearts and homes. They have done this as much by their hard work as they have with their loyalty and affection.

People learned to breed dogs to bring out specific traits in them. Selective breeding created dogs that were excellent at various jobs, from herding to finding and bringing back game for hunters.

Today trainers have found ways to use dogs to locate criminals, sniff out drugs and explosives, and even help people with disabilities get around in our high-tech world.

Dogs' physical traits have made them reliable workers for thousands of years, while their devotion has made them trusted companions. What new jobs will these canine helpers do for us in the next century?

Words to Know

Breed   A group of animals within a species. Humans try to let only animals of a selected size, color, and shape be born within a breed.

Canine   Of or relating to the dog family.

Carnivore   Animals, especially members of the dog, cat, bear, and weasel family, that feed on the flesh of other animals.

Guide Dog   A dog that leads and helps a person who has a visual disability; sometimes known as a "Seeing Eye Dog," a term trademarked by Seeing Eye, Inc., of Morristown, New Jersey.

K-9   Short for canine.

Mongrel   *See* mixed breed.

Mixed Breed   A dog whose mother and father were not of the same breed. Also called a mutt.

Purebred   A dog whose mother and father and other relatives were all of the same breed.

Schutzhund   A German word meaning "protection dog."

SAR   Search and rescue.

Service Dog   A dog such as a guide dog or assistance dog. A service dog is not kept as a pet.

Therapy   Any procedure designed to heal or cure an illness or disorder.

Working Dog   A dog such as a sheepdog or retriever. A working dog is not kept as a pet.

INDEX

actors, 43
aggression, 10
American Kennel Club, 45
attack dogs, 10

blind people. *See* guide dogs.
bloodhounds 15, 16
bulldogs, 43
breeding dogs, 5, 46

Dalmatians, 30
deaf people. *See* signal dogs.
disaster search, 16
disposition, 15
dog shows, 45
dogsledding, 18, 20

eye, 22

greyhounds, 32
guide dogs, 34, 37, 38, 46
guard dogs, 6, 10, 46

herding dogs, 22, 46
Homeward Bound, 43
hunting dogs, 27, 29

instinct and training, 22, 24
Iditarod Trail Sled Dog Race, 20

K-9 units, 6

law enforcement, 6, 9, 10

obedience training, 6, 10
101 Dalmatians, 43

pets, 5, 27, 29, 38, 46
pointers 27
police dogs, 6, 9, 10

racing dogs, 32
retrievers, 27

sense of smell, 9, 12, 15, 16, 27
Schutzhund, 10
search and rescue (SAR), 12, 16, 46
Seeing Eye dogs, *see* guide dogs.
sighthounds, 32
signal dogs, 40, 46
speed, 32
sheepdogs, 22, 24, 46
sheepdog trials, 26
sled dogs, 18, 20
snowmobiles, 18

therapy dogs, 42
tracking and trailing, 12, 15
traits, 5, 9, 12, 18, 22, 24, 27, 30, 37, 40, 42, 46

trust, 6, 37, 38, 40

wolves as ancestors, 5

Cover Photo: Gary Shultz (The Wildlife Collection).
Photo Credits: Norvia Behling (Behling and Johnson Photography), pages 8, 14, 25, 28, 31, 44; Florent Flipper (Unicorn Stock Photos), page 39; Michael Francis (The Wildlife Collection), page 23; Jean Higgins (Unicorn Stock Photos), page 36; Martin Harvey (The Wildlife Collection), page 7; Fred D. Jordan (Unicorn Stock Photos), page 11; Marie Mills (Unicorn Stock Photos), page 13; Alon Reininger (Unicorn Stock Photos), page 4; Gary Shultz (The Wildlife Collection), page 19; Lynn M. Stone, page 17; SuperStock, Inc., pages 33, 35, 41; Dick Young (Unicorn Stock Photos), page 21.